Understand

WOMEN'S
HEALTH

**Dr Malcolm Griffiths
& Dr Kay E Elliott**

Published by Family Doctor Publications
in association with the British Medical Association

IMPORTANT

This book is intended not as a substitute for personal medical advice but as a supplement to that advice for the patient who wishes to understand more about his or her condition.

Before taking any form of treatment YOU SHOULD ALWAYS CONSULT YOUR MEDICAL PRACTITIONER.

In particular (without limit) you should note that advances in medical science occur rapidly and some of the information about drugs and treatment contained in this booklet may very soon be out of date.

© Family Doctor Publications 1996, 1999, 2001
Updated 2001

Family Doctor Publications, PO BOX 4664, Poole, Dorset BH15 1NN

Medical Editor: Dr Tony Smith
Consultant Editor: Kathleen Lyle
Cover Artist: Dave Eastbury
Medical Artist: Angela Christie
Design: Fox Design, Bramley, Guildford, Surrey
Printing: Reflex Litho, Thetford, using acid-free paper

ISBN: 1 898205 95 7

Contents

Introduction

This book is intended to give background information on aspects of women's health with details about what can go wrong and why, as well as advice on treatment. Many aspects of women's health, not just those directly connected with reproduction, may differ from men's. Patterns of disease and provision of care are different for the two sexes, for instance the detection and treatment of depression. We have concentrated on problems relating to reproduction and the reproductive organs, because this is our field of expertise, but we accept that there are many other issues outside the scope of this book. We hope that armed with suitable information women will be able to seek the help they need from other health professionals.

On average women tend to consult doctors more frequently than men. There are many reasons for this – it is women who get pregnant, and who take a disproportionate responsibility for contraception and for caring for children and other family members. Unfortunately, problems occur more frequently with the workings of the female reproductive organs than with male ones.

Traditionally medicine has (like other professions) been male dominated. This has caused a lack of understanding of women's problems by doctors, or at least a perception by women that there is a lack of understanding. The increasing availability of women doctors (both GPs and specialists) will help this problem, but it is also important for women to appreciate that very many male doctors can offer the necessary support, advice and treatment.

This booklet is aimed at women of all ages. Problems that arise in childhood are covered, as well as those that happen after the menopause. The topics are arranged chronologically as far as possible, but obviously some of the themes run throughout life. Problems that can occur in pregnancy have not been addressed because they are dealt with in the booklet *Understanding Pregnancy*. There are also other books in the series: *Understanding the Menopause and HRT*, *Understanding Breast Disorders* and *Understanding Infertility* (to be published). We hope the book will be useful as a family reference.

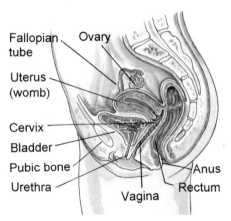

Fallopian tube
Ovary
Uterus (womb)
Cervix
Bladder
Pubic bone
Urethra
Anus
Rectum
Vagina

The reproductive organs and the bladder

Childhood – before puberty

VAGINAL DISCHARGE

It is common for newborn girls to have some vaginal secretions soon after birth and while they are being breast-fed. This is caused by a small amount of the mother's sex hormones which pass to the daughter. Once breast-feeding is over then any vaginal discharge is abnormal until the girl reaches puberty. Discharge may be obvious or may only be noticed as a staining of the gusset of a girl's underwear. Persistent vaginal discharge in a girl before puberty should be reported to your family doctor for investigation and treatment.

PRECOCIOUS PUBERTY

The average age at which the changes of puberty begin (also called the menarche) is about 10 to 13. When those changes begin much earlier, this is referred to as precocious puberty. Occasionally it may be a variation of normal, but if breast development begins before the age of eight, or periods before

CAUSES OF VAGINAL DISCHARGE

- Objects inserted into the vagina during play (may include sweets, seeds and small toys)
- Threadworm infection

- (usually coming from the back passage)
- Thrush (see section on common infections – page 37)
- Related to sexual abuse

ten, then it should always be reported to your family doctor, who will probably refer the girl to a specialist. Where puberty occurs very early it is generally caused by overactive hormone production and usually requires specialist treatment to prevent long-term problems affecting growth and sexual development.

DELAYED PUBERTY

If there is no breast development by the age of 13, or periods do not start, this may also need specialist investigation and advice.

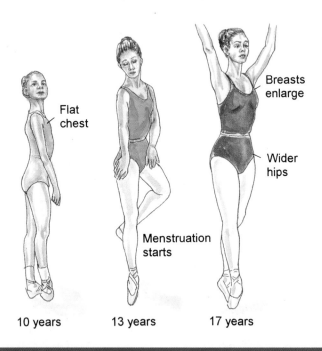

Flat chest

Breasts enlarge

Wider hips

Menstruation starts

10 years   13 years   17 years

KEY POINTS

✓ For newborn babies, some vaginal discharge is normal

✓ Vaginal discharge is not normal for girls before puberty

✓ Periods usually start between the ages of 10 and 13

Teens – menarche and puberty

MENSTRUAL CYCLE – PHYSIOLOGY AND ANATOMY

The time during which a girl goes through her development into an adult to sexual maturity is called puberty. This phase is made up of a variety of overlapping events and developments. Physical changes such as breast development, hair growth and onset of periods are combined with emotional and psychological changes which are less obvious from the outside but nevertheless important. Menarche is the medical term for the onset of periods.

The activity of the sexual organs, including their development in the teens, is under the control of a small gland at the base of the brain – the pituitary gland. This gland produces chemical messengers (hormones), which in turn control the activity of other hormone-producing glands in the body – the thyroid gland, ovaries or testicles, and adrenal glands.

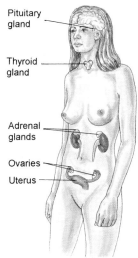

Control of development of hormone production

Two of the hormones from the pituitary gland are follicle-stimulating hormone (FSH) and luteinising hormone (LH). Basically in women FSH encourages the development of small follicles (like tiny blisters) on the surface of the ovaries. These follicles contain the eggs. More than one follicle may start to develop at a time but usually only one reaches maturity each month. While the follicle is developing, the cells around the egg produce one of the female hormones – oestrogen.

Oestrogen has a variety of effects and is largely responsible for the changes which occur in young women around puberty. It produces breast development, hair growth and so on. Each month it causes the lining of the womb (the endometrium) to grow and prepare the cavity of the womb or uterus to receive a fertilised egg.

creates a corpus luteum and now starts to produce the second female hormone – progesterone.

Progesterone affects the growth and function of the breasts, and stabilises the thickened lining of the womb to make it more receptive to a fertilised egg. If an egg has been fertilised it implants and grows within the lining of the womb. This implanted embryo produces another hormone – human chorionic gonadotrophin – which tells the ovary to continue to produce progesterone – helping to stabilise the lining of the womb.

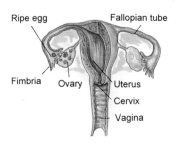

Female internal organs

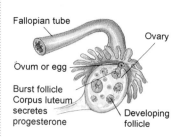

Egg release from an ovary

Once the follicle has reached a certain size and development, the rising level of oestrogen in the blood signals to the pituitary that the ovary is ready to release the egg. The pituitary then sends out a high level of the second hormone (LH). This signals the ovary to release the egg. The cluster of cells which had formed the follicle

If no fertilised egg implants then there is no message to maintain progesterone production. After a few days the cells of the corpus luteum stop producing hormones. The levels of oestrogen and progesterone fall, the lining of the womb starts to break up and the top layer is shed as the period. Periods, often irregular in the first few months, are the loss of blood together with some of the lining of the womb each month. This is lost through the vagina.

These changes will happen like this only in normal sexual organs. The pictures will help you to understand how they look.

You can see that the uterus (womb) sits above the vagina, with the cervix protruding down to where you can probably feel it if you put your finger inside. About a third of women have a womb that tips backwards (referred to as retroverted) rather than forwards (called anteverted) – either is quite normal. The fallopian tubes are connected on either side to the womb and produce a passage for the eggs to pass from the ovary towards the womb. Fertilisation by sperm after sexual intercourse usually happens in the tubes. The two ovaries (close to the ends of the tubes) are attached to the side of the womb by ligaments.

NORMAL SEXUAL DEVELOPMENT

For girls, sexual development usually starts at around the age of 10 (see page 3). The levels of hormones that govern development of body hair, breast growth and the onset of periods (and which later control menstruation and reproduction) gradually increase over a few months. Often the first sign that

girls notice is the growth of a small tender pea-sized swelling under one nipple. This is known as a breast bud. As it grows another will appear on the other side. This is the beginning of adult breast development.

Coarse dark body hair begins to grow in the armpits and over the pubic area, and sometimes up towards the navel.

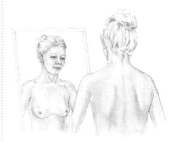

DELAYS IN SEXUAL DEVELOPMENT

There is a wide range of ages during which puberty and sexual development may take place. Sometimes if puberty (or one or more aspect of sexual development) is early or delayed it can cause worries. Very early development is discussed in the section on childhood. Delays can be of concern too. Almost always there is no underlying problem; quite simply, we all develop at different rates. Very rarely sexual development is delayed beyond the age of 13 and in such situations a girl and her family may need to consult their GP for reassurance and possibly referral for specialist advice.

There is a condition in which all stages of sexual development occur as expected, but periods don't appear. Sometimes a girl experiences some monthly lower abdominal pain, which can become more and more severe. In this condition there is a complete membrane over the vaginal opening (known as an imperforate hymen) and this causes a build-up of menstrual loss in the vagina each month. Eventually it is necessary to make a small hole in the hymen to relieve the discomfort and allow normal periods each month.

Other causes for delayed sexual development include hormonal and (very rare) congenital abnormalities of the womb and reproductive organs. Such problems need specialist advice.

KEY POINTS

✓ Normal sexual development for girls usually starts at about the age of ten

✓ Hormones are chemical messengers, which program organs of the body to behave in certain ways

✓ Menstruation is a complex process involving several different hormones

CONCEPTION

Conception is the fusion of female egg with male sperm, and requires a number of events.

Failures in this series of processes are discussed in the section on fertility treatment.

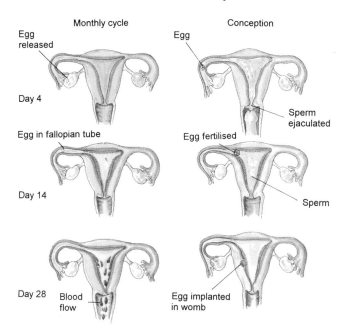

Monthly cycle	Conception
Egg released	Egg
Day 4	Sperm ejaculated
Egg in fallopian tube	Egg fertilised
Day 14	Sperm
Day 28 Blood flow	Egg implanted in womb

Process of conception

CONCEPTION – THE SEQUENCE OF EVENTS

1 The ovary must release one or more eggs (ovulation)
2 Fertile active sperm must be released into the vagina (usually during intercourse)
3 At least one sperm and egg must meet up (via the fallopian tubes) and fuse

CONTRACEPTION

Women may be fertile from shortly before their first period until their last one. Pregnancy may follow unprotected intercourse at any time in the menstrual cycle. If contraception is not used, about 40 out of 100 sexually active women will become pregnant within a year. It is useful when comparing different methods of contraception to compare their effectiveness with this figure of 40 in 100 in mind. The type of contraception that suits a particular woman may vary over her reproductive life.

Confidential family planning advice is available free, from most family doctors, family planning clinics, youth advice clinics and Brook Advisory clinics (these three are in the phone directory, Yellow Pages and Thomson Local Directory). You can find more detailed information about contraceptive methods in leaflets available from the Family Planning Association – see Useful addresses on page 66.

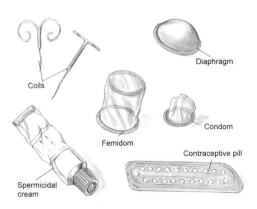

Coils

Diaphragm

Femidom

Condom

Contraceptive pill

Spermicidal cream

Contraceptives available

NON-HORMONAL METHODS

Withdrawal (coitus interruptus)

In this widely practised method, the man withdraws his penis before he ejaculates ('comes').

Rhythm method

This method relies on predicting the most fertile time of the month. It is helpful only if your cycles are regular and you and your partner are self-disciplined and well motivated. It is based on one or a combination of observations over several cycles:

- temperature charts
- characteristic of cervical mucus
- diary of periods.

Specially trained family planning nurses can advise.

Sheaths (condoms)

A fine rubber sheath is rolled over the erect penis before penetration.

Condoms ('french letters') are available from many sources (pharmacies, supermarkets, family planning clinics). Durex and Mates are well-known brands.

Female condom (Femidom)

This is made of polyurethane. It is larger than a male condom. It lines the vagina and covers the vulva, and can be held in place by a plastic ring which fits into the vagina.

Spermicides

These are chemicals that kill sperm. They can come in the form of creams, jellies, pessaries or 'C-film'. They are relatively inexpensive, and they can increase the effectiveness of other methods (particularly withdrawal and barrier methods such as condoms, caps and diaphragms).

Many brands of condom are lubricated with a spermicide which makes them more effective (and may protect against HIV). Spermicides are not effective enough to be used alone, except in the first year after the menopause when contraception is still advised.

IUCDs/'coils'

Intrauterine contraceptive devices (IUCDs) are small devices made of plastic, plastic and copper, or more recently plastic with a hormone-releasing core, which are inserted into the womb by a family planning doctor.

Where heavy periods are likely to occur the hormone-releasing IUCD (Mirena) may be the appropriate one to use.

The presence of a coil inside the womb stops a fertilised egg settling and growing. The copper, present in many modern coils, helps with this effect and means that the devices can be small, minimising the side effects of heavier periods.

NON-HORMONAL METHODS
WITHDRAWAL METHOD

Advantages
- Under the couple's control
- No medical input needed

Disadvantages
- Very unreliable
- Sperms are present in the fluid from the penis before ejaculation
- Sperms spilt on the outside may find their way into the vagina
- The man may misjudge the moment to withdraw

RHYTHM METHOD

Advantages
- Specialist help only needed to learn the method
- Acceptable to the Roman Catholic church

Disadvantages
- Failure rates may be high (up to 20 pregnancies per 100 women per year)
- Limits opportunities for sex

SHEATH METHOD

Advantages
- Cheap
- Offer some protection from sexually transmitted diseases (STDs) and human immunodeficiency virus (HIV)
- Can be used in addition to other contraceptive methods for STD/HIV protection ('double Dutch')

Disadvantages
- Interrupts the act of sex
- Failure rate may be as low as two per 100 women per year, but average figure is higher

FEMALE CONDOM

Advantages
- Can be inserted before sex
- Even more protection against STDs than male condoms
- Under the woman's control
- No interference with menstrual cycle or periods
- Allergies do not occur – compare latex condoms

Disadvantages
- More expensive than male condoms
- Failure rate may be high

Advantages

- Very effective (about two pregnancies per 100 women per year)
- May be left in place for three to eight years (depending on model)
- The progestogen-releasing coil will ease heavy periods as well as providing contraception

Disadvantages

- Fitting is like a prolonged smear test examination, and may be uncomfortable
- Periods may be more troublesome (painful/heavy)

HORMONAL METHODS

Combined oral contraceptive pill (COCP)

These pills contain a combination of oestrogen and progesterone, and are taken daily for 21 days out of 28. They work by preventing ovulation.

Progesterone-only pill (POP, 'mini-pill')

These pills contain progesterone alone. They are taken every day, with no pill-free interval. They work by thickening mucus in the cervix so that sperm cannot reach the eggs. They are almost as effective as the combined pill if no pills are missed, and they can be useful at times when the combined pill is not suitable, such as during breast-feeding. Breast-feeding has some contraceptive effect, but it is unpredictable and unreliable.

Progesterone injection (DepoProvera, Depostat)

An injection of progesterone is given every two or three months. The hormone is slowly released and prevents ovulation.

Progesterone implant (Norplant)

Six soft plastic tubes (the size of matchsticks) are inserted under the skin, on the underside of the upper arm, under local anaesthetic. The progesterone is released slowly and prevents ovulation.

STERILISATION

Sterilisation of the woman is the most reliable form of contraception; it is irreversible and should be contemplated only if a woman is certain that her family is complete. It is usually performed under a general anaesthetic, although a local

HORMONAL METHODS

COMBINED PILL

Advantages
- Very effective (failure rate of about one pregnancy per 100 women per year)
- May help regulate periods or lessen heavy periods and reduce period pain

Disadvantages
- Must be prescription only
- May not be suitable for all
- Have to be taken every day
- A small risk of abnormal blood clotting (thrombosis), especially in women over 35 and those who smoke

PROGESTERONE-ONLY PILL

Advantages
- Quite effective (though less so than the combined pill)
- Can be taken while breast-feeding
- Can be taken by women who can't take the combined pill

Disadvantages
- Must be prescribed by a doctor
- Periods sometimes become irregular

PROGESTERONE INJECTION

Advantages
- Extremely effective
- Given by a nurse or doctor
- Once given you don't have to do anything else – you can forget about contraception until the next injection

Disadvantages
- Initially periods may become irregular, and usually after the second injection they stop completely – which concerns some users
- Any side effects may persist for months

PROGESTERONE IMPLANT

Advantages
- Extremely effective
- Works for five years

Disadvantages
- Insertion and removal need a specially trained doctor
- Periods often become irregular

anaesthetic is available in some units. The fallopian tubes are divided either by cutting them or cauterising or, most commonly, by applying a plastic clip or ring. This can usually be done with only two small cuts about one centimetre long on the abdomen, using a telescopic device to see the tubes and apply clips.

Some women, particularly if overweight, may need a small open operation to allow the surgeon to see the tubes.

Sterilisation is usually done as a separate procedure, but in some circumstances may be performed at the same time as an abortion, or at the same time as a caesarean section.

FERTILITY TREATMENT

Fertilisation may fail to occur for a variety of reasons (see box).

Doctors usually consider it appropriate to investigate and treat couples who fail to get pregnant after a year or more of trying. Some couples may be concerned about a failure sooner. If you consult your family doctor before a year is up, he or she will generally reassure you that you are likely to conceive spontaneously. Depending on local circumstances, expertise and knowledge of your medical history, your family doctor may do some basic tests or refer you to a specialist.

If there is anovulation (i.e. no eggs are released), your family doctor or specialist may advise treatment with tablets containing clomiphene (Clomid, Serophene). This is usually taken for five days at the start of each cycle. It helps to improve the chances of ovulation occurring. There is a small risk that it can cause the release of more than one egg, resulting in twins or triplets. Occasionally it can also cause ovarian cysts. If clomiphene doesn't work, other forms of assisted conception using injection treatment to induce ovulation may be

REASONS FOR INFERTILITY

- Bad luck (it may be good luck if unprotected intercourse takes place when a pregnancy is not planned!)
- Not having intercourse at the right time
- Failure of egg production
- Failure of sperm production or function
- Anything which prevents the sperm and egg meeting up – such as blocked or damaged fallopian tubes

BASIC TESTS

Sperm test
The man produces a sample of semen by masturbation. This is taken to a laboratory, where a microscope is used to assess the quality and sperm count of the sample

Hormone tests
Blood taken from the woman (usually around day 21 of her cycle) may show a raised level of progesterone – confirming that ovulation has occurred. Other hormone tests may reveal other causes for anovulation (failure of ovulation)

Temperature chart
You may be asked to keep an accurate record of your temperature at the start of each day. If ovulation occurs there is a small rise in the body temperature due to the raised level of progesterone. On the same chart, mark your period days and times when you had intercourse

needed. The dose of these injections needs to be closely monitored by either ultrasound scans or blood and urine tests to minimise the risks of twins or triplets or problems with ovarian cysts. Rarely if many eggs begin to develop the course of injections may be abandoned for safety, giv-ing a lower dose in a subsequent cycle. Treatment of sperm problems is difficult and is likely to require specialist help. The fallopian tubes can be assessed by two methods (some specialists use both, others just one or the other).

● **Hysterosalpingogram** – during an examination like a smear test a tube is attached to the cervix. Special dye is injected through the tube, which shows up on X-rays; the shape of the inside of the womb and tubes and spillage of the dye from the ends of the tubes can be seen on X-rays.

● **Laparoscopy and dye test** – done under a general anaesthetic. A telescope is inserted into the abdominal cavity, below the umbilicus. The gynaecologist uses it to see the pelvic organs. Dye is injected through a tube attached to the cervix and can be seen spilling from the ends of the tubes, if they are not blocked.

If tubes are blocked, then in order to allow conception to take place either tubal surgery or in vitro fertilisation is needed. Both of these usually need special expertise. Blockage is usually due to past infection, endometriosis (see page 29) or previous operations:

- **Tubal surgery** involves a general anaesthetic. It is usually done through a cut across the lower abdomen ('bikini scar'). Scar tissue is broken down and normal anatomy restored as far as possible.
- **In vitro fertilisation** uses drug treatment to stimulate egg production; this is monitored by ultrasound scans. When the eggs are ready to be released the gynaecologist collects them using a fine needle. In the laboratory they are then mixed with sperm and fertilisation takes place. Once the fertilised eggs have started to grow and divide they are put into the womb via a tube inserted through the cervix.

In women with tubes that aren't blocked, a simpler procedure may be used. Eggs are collected and mixed with sperm, which are then injected into the tubes together. This technique, called GIFT (**g**amete **i**ntra-**f**allopian tube **t**ransfer), is used in 'unexplained infertility'.

POLYCYSTIC OVARIES

This disorder is not well understood. The ovaries tend to be a little larger than average and contain a number of very small cysts under the surface. There are different degrees of the condition. The presence of poly- cystic ovaries, associated with some or all of the problems that they may cause, is referred to as poly-cystic ovarian syndrome. Problems which this syndrome may cause are:

- excessive weight
- infertility
- infrequent or absent periods
- male pattern baldness
- hirsutism (excessive body hair growth)
- greasy skin and acne.

How polycystic ovarian syndrome is treated will depend on the woman's particular circumstances and needs. Treatment could be one of the following:

- dietary advice to help weight reduction
- fertility treatment
- the contraceptive pill
- special contraceptive pills to improve the hormonal balance (Dianette)
- ovarian diathermy – using laparoscopy, electricity is used to produce small burns on the ovarian surface.

TERMINATION OF PREGNANCY

The word abortion medically means a miscarriage. In common use, though, an abortion means a therapeutic miscarriage where the

METHODS OF ABORTION

'Medical abortion': the woman takes a tablet (Mifegyne) and 36–48 hours later a second drug (Cervagem) is given as a vaginal tablet. Following this the woman miscarries. This method can be used only up to nine weeks of pregnancy

Suction termination of pregnancy: usually carried out under a general anaesthetic. The cervix is gently stretched to allow insertion of a suction tube into the cavity of the womb, to remove the pregnancy (that is fetus, placenta and membranes). It is usually possible up to about 14 weeks of pregnancy

Prostaglandin-induced abortion: drugs called prostaglandins are given to induce a miscarriage. The drugs may be given as an injection into the womb, as a solution injected through the cervix, or these days most commonly as a vaginal tablet (Cervagem)

Dilatation and extraction: under a general anaesthetic and usually after a single dose of prostaglandin, the cervix is again gently stretched, sufficient to allow the passage of forceps which are used to grasp and remove the pregnancy in pieces. The last two methods may be used up to about 22 weeks, and exceptionally (for congenital abnormalities incompatible with life) later still

pregnancy is ended intentionally. An abortion may legally be performed in the United Kingdom (excluding Northern Ireland) under a number of circumstances defined by the 1967 Abortion Act, modified by subsequent legislation. Effectively an abortion may be performed if:

- there is a significant risk to the woman's life or physical or mental health

- there is a significant risk to the health of her existing children
- there is a substantial risk that the unborn child might be severely handicapped.

Pregnancy is now regarded as being almost universally safe, but it has been statistically proved that an early termination of pregnancy is safer than allowing even an uncomplicated pregnancy to continue to full term. This has allowed a very flexible interpretation of the law, so that 'abortion on demand' is almost the rule. Many terminations of pregnancy are performed on the grounds of risk to the woman's psychological well-being. In practice almost any woman with an early unplanned pregnancy will be able to obtain a termination of pregnancy.

The earlier a termination is performed the lower the risk of complications. There is little or no evidence that early termination of pregnancy affects a woman's chances of having successful pregnancies in the future. Some women may feel uncomfortable about termination of pregnancy. It is also possible to seek help through local family planning clinics (see your telephone directory) or via pregnancy counselling services (Marie Stopes Organisation, PAS – see Useful addresses). Termination of pregnancy is offered when tests performed in early pregnancy diagnose an abnormality in the fetus. The method of termination of pregnancy depends on:

- the stage of pregnancy reached
- the woman's wishes
- facilities and expertise available
- medical considerations.

After any type of termination of pregnancy there is a risk of some tissue being left behind, or infection of the womb lining occurring. In such cases the woman may experience heavy bleeding, pain or fever. She should report these symptoms to her doctors, who may treat her with antibiotics or a further operation to remove any remaining tissue.

KEY POINTS

✓ Many methods of contraception are available – the same one will not suit everybody

✓ There are many reasons for infertility and many ways of treating it

✓ Termination of pregnancy (abortion) is legal in the United Kingdom under certain conditions

Period problems

PREMENSTRUAL TENSION AND PREMENSTRUAL SYNDROME

Premenstrual tension (PMT) is the cyclical occurrence of symptoms such as depression, moodiness or anxiety, which most women experience to a greater or lesser extent in the days leading up to their period. For some women it is non-existent or so minor that it doesn't constitute a problem, but for other women it can become disabling.

When PMT is associated with other marked premenstrual symptoms, such as breast discomfort, abdominal swelling (bloating), abdominal pain or fluid retention, it is called premenstrual syndrome (PMS).

Premenstrual symptoms, both physical and psychological, may be more difficult to cope with when a woman also has a degree of depression; in this situation, treating the underlying depression may also improve the premenstrual syndrome.

Another suggestion is that women who experience PMS/PMT are generally more stressed and that like all women they are more susceptible to the results of such stress just before their period.

There is no evidence that any of these explanations is the correct one. It is more than likely that any one of the three explanations may apply in different cases. Although most of the research in this area has concentrated on an imbalance between the two female hormones oestrogen and progesterone – particularly a deficiency of the latter – there is no objective evidence to support this explanation.

If you have PMT or PMS it is certainly worth trying to keep a diary to record symptoms, timing of periods and any stressful events at home, at work or in relationships. To be sure that PMS/PMT is the cause, you should notice at least a relief from symptoms in the week after your period.

TREATMENTS

● Stress avoidance and relaxation techniques are useful – particularly during the premenstrual phase, but ideally throughout the cycle. Get a good night's

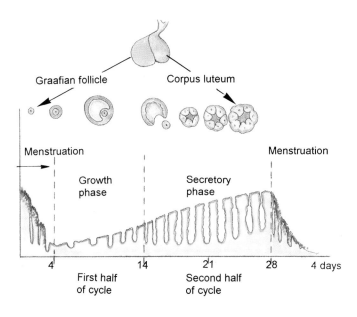

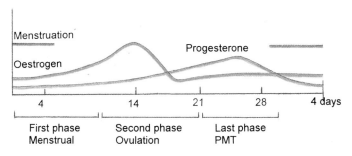

Relationship of hormonal changes to development of a fertile egg. **Top**: development of egg; **middle**: changes in the lining of the womb; **bottom**: hormonal control of both processes

sleep, take time out to exercise and relax, get support from your partner and family.

- Vitamin B_6 and preparations based on evening primrose oil may be helpful.
- Hormone replacement therapy (HRT) may also help.

Where symptoms of PMT/PMS are severe, an operation may be the answer. If a woman has completed her family or if there are other indications for hysterectomy, a hysterectomy with removal of both ovaries (hysterectomy and bilateral salpingo-oophorectomy) may be suggested.

This removes the source of the cyclical hormone changes, so it is very effective. After this operation the woman will need to take non-cyclical HRT (oestrogen only) at least until the age of 50.

ABSENT OR INFREQUENT PERIODS

Although periods are often seen as a nuisance, it can be worrying when they don't come. A delay in the initial onset of periods is dealt with in the section on Teens (see page 7). Where periods have become established and then are missed, there are several possible explanations.

If your periods are absent or infrequent you usually want reassurance that there is nothing serious

HORMONE TREATMENT FOR PMT/PMS

Progestogens: taken as a supplement in the premenstrual phase – need to be taken as suppositories

Combined contraceptive pill: theoreticaaly ought to remove cyclical changes in hormones, but does so in some women although not all

Contraceptive injection/implant: temporarily completely removes cyclical changes

Hormone replacement therapy (HRT): very suitable for women approaching the menopause with PMS/PMT symptoms

wrong. Your family doctor may need to arrange a simple blood test to make a diagnosis or exclude serious problems.

If you are trying for a baby, fertility treatment may be appropriate. If premature menopause is diagnosed long-term HRT will be necessary. Particularly in a young woman who has not completed her family, counselling and specialist referral for fertility treatment may be needed. Eating disorders and other causes of major weight loss need

Pregnancy: if you were trying for a baby, this is good news. If not, you should consult your family doctor or family planning clinic as soon as possible

Failure of ovulation: the ovaries aren't releasing an egg each month, so there is no hormonal cycle and the lining of the womb (endometrium) doesn't grow and shed normally

Menopause: this can happen at almost any age; for most women it occurs from the mid-forties onwards. A woman experiencing an early (premature) menopause should always consult her family doctor, who may refer her to a specialist. Some women may wish to consider hormone replacement therapy

Significant weight loss: women who have eating disorders such as anorexia nervosa and those who are underweight through strenuous exercise lose too much body fat, which affects the production of hormones and ovulation

Polycystic ovarian syndrome: in this condition (see page 17) the production of ovarian hormones and eggs may be blocked

A benign (non-cancerous) tumour of the pituitary gland at the base of the brain can produce excessive levels of the hormone prolactin, which blocks ovarian activity

specific treatment. For any woman who misses her periods for many months, a blood test may be needed to ensure adequate levels of hormones as long-term deficiency of female hormones can have a harmful effect on bones, blood vessels and the heart.

PAINFUL PERIODS

The medical term for painful periods is dysmenorrhoea, which may be present from menarche (primary dysmenorrhoea) or occur from some later time (secondary dysmenorrhoea). In practice this separation is not very useful. Similarly the pattern or timing of the pain, separated into pain that starts before bleeding (congestive) and pain that starts with the onset of bleeding (spasmodic), only occasionally gives a clue to the underlying cause.

Most women experience some pain or discomfort with periods. The severity will vary considerably among women even in the absence of any underlying disorder.

Such pain is usually treated with painkillers, non-steroidal anti-inflammatory drugs being the most widely prescribed (see page 25).

If this is ineffective, hormonal treatment may be given to stop ovulation.

Severe pain may also result from one of the following specific conditions:

- endometriosis
- adenomyosis
- pelvic congestion syndrome
- fibroids.

In these conditions treatment will be with drugs or surgery according to the specific disorder.

HEAVY OR FREQUENT PERIODS

Periods may be:

- heavy
- prolonged
- too frequent
- infrequent
- painful.

Doctors used to use Greek and Latin terms to describe these patterns, for example, menorrhagia meant heavy periods. These terms were of some value when it was thought that particular patterns of menstruation were associated with specific disorders. We no longer think this is the case, so it is more appropriate to use English words to describe the problem in a way that everyone can understand.

Heavy and frequent periods often occur together. The length of the normal menstrual cycle is very variable, from woman to woman and cycle to cycle in the same woman. A cycle shorter than 21 days from the first day of one period to the first day of the next is usually regarded as abnormal.

Nevertheless a woman may find any interval of less than 28 days a nuisance. Assessing the amount of blood lost with the period is extremely difficult. Unless it results in a low blood count (anaemia), the messy procedure of saving used sanitary protection and extracting the blood in the laboratory is the only way of objectively measuring the heaviness of periods. Where such tests are done (usually only in research studies), up to 80 millilitres of blood loss is usually regarded as normal.

Many women who feel that their periods are heavy lose less than 80 millilitres. Drug treatments which are effective for heavy periods are most effective for women who have a loss of more than 80 millilitres each period. Nevertheless it is generally the woman's perception of blood loss which is relevant, and that is what needs to be treated.

Drug treatment

The woman's circumstances will indicate the most appropriate therapy. In order of effectiveness, the drugs used are:

- **Contraceptive pill**: the combined pill is very effective and suitable for women who also need contraception.
- **Drugs** that help block the production of chemicals in the lining of the uterus which in turn interfere with the clotting of blood (tranexamic acid or Cyclokapron).
- **Non-steroidal anti-inflammatory drugs** (**NSAIDs**): the most widely prescribed is mefenamic acid (Ponstan). They work by helping break up blood clots and aiding production of prostaglandins, which are chemicals that affect blood vessels in the endometrium. This type of drug is also effective against period pain.
- **Hormone replacement therapy** (**HRT**): particularly useful in older women who experience heavy or irregular periods leading up to the menopause.
- **Drugs to stop bleeding** from blood vessels in the endometrium (ethamsylate or Dicynene)
- **Progestogens** (medroxyprogesterone, norethisterone, didrogesterone): the most frequently used drugs. They are commonly given for 7 to 10 days in the second half of the cycle, but there is little evidence that they work when given in this way.

If they are to be effective they probably need to be given for 21 days in every 28. They are more likely to be effective if the cycle is short or irregular.

Surgical treatment

It is the endometrium that bleeds each month, so an operation that removes the endometrium will abolish periods. Traditionally this has involved removing the whole womb (hysterectomy). The womb can be removed vaginally, without any cut on the abdomen (vaginal hysterectomy), or through an incision on the abdomen (abdominal hysterectomy).

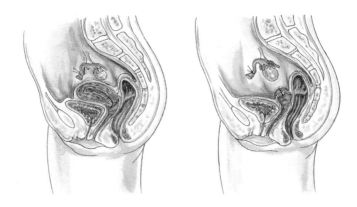

Internal organs before and after hysterectomy

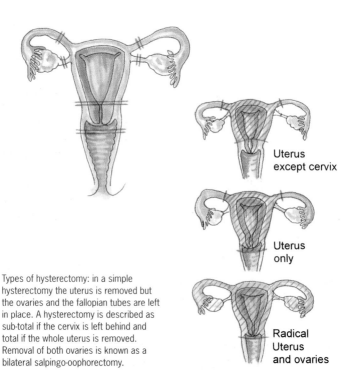

Uterus except cervix

Uterus only

Radical Uterus and ovaries

Types of hysterectomy: in a simple hysterectomy the uterus is removed but the ovaries and the fallopian tubes are left in place. A hysterectomy is described as sub-total if the cervix is left behind and total if the whole uterus is removed. Removal of both ovaries is known as a bilateral salpingo-oophorectomy.

Either of these can be combined with removal of the ovaries and tubes (bilateral salpingo-oophorectomy), although the combination is more common with abdominal hysterectomy. This operation is usually indicated where there is some ovarian disorder as well. It may be appropriate in older women too, but increasingly it is being offered to younger women as it avoids the risk of any subsequent ovarian disorder. In this case HRT is needed long term. The method for hysterectomy is influenced by:

- the surgeon's preference and expertise
- the presence or absence of prolapse (see page 36)
- previous gynaecological surgery or caesarean section
- the size of the womb
- whether the ovaries and tubes are to be removed also (usually difficult at vaginal hysterectomy).

Increasingly gynaecologists are performing hysterectomies vaginally, as this method is usually associated with a quicker recovery and less chance of complications. Shorter and shorter stays are the order of the day – especially with vaginal hysterectomy where the stay in hospital may be only 48 hours. The use of minimally invasive surgical techniques (keyhole surgery) has produced two new surgical approaches to heavy periods – endometrial resection/ablation and laparoscopically assisted hysterectomy.

- In endometrial resection/ablation a viewing tube (hysteroscope) is passed into the womb through the cervix. Surgical instruments attached to the hysteroscope are used to remove the endometrium lining the womb, using either diathermy (electricity), laser energy or microwaves. If all of the endometrium can be removed or destroyed, the result will be no more periods, but without the problems or risk of complications of major surgery. Unfortunately it is not possible to guarantee this outcome, which may limit the value of such surgery in individual cases. Many women still prefer the certainty of hysterectomy.
- Laparoscopically assisted hysterectomy involves exactly the same steps as conventional abdominal hysterectomy but these are carried out via a series of small abdominal incisions using instruments controlled by the surgeon guided by a telescope inserted below the navel (umbilicus). At the end of the operation the womb (with or without the ovaries and tubes) is removed

through the vagina. Effectively the advantage of this new form of surgery is to allow a vaginal hysterectomy to be performed in circumstances where an abdominal hysterectomy would otherwise be needed. Rarely, major complications can occur.

Before you decide to undergo such surgery you should discuss your expectations and any possible complications with your family doctor and gynaecologist – and probably also ask about your gynaecologist's experience of these procedures.

KEY POINTS

✓ PMS/PMT can be a severe problem for some women, but treatment is available

✓ Periods that are irregular or unduly heavy can cause inconvenience and concern

✓ Treatment may be by drugs or by operation

✓ Self-help is always worth a try

Pain with intercourse

Pain in the lower abdomen, deep pelvic pain and pelvic pain experienced during sexual intercourse (deep dyspareunia) are often, quite logically, assumed to be gynaecological in origin. In fact other organs lie low in the abdomen and pelvis and can cause such symptoms.

It may be necessary to examine these other organs or to arrange

special tests to exclude problems with them.

Pelvic and lower abdominal pain may be caused by several conditions which are dealt with elsewhere in this book.

ENDOMETRIOSIS

The womb is lined with tissue called endometrium (see the figure on page 30). Part of the endometrium is shed each month as the period (or 'withdrawal bleed' in women taking the contraceptive pill).

For reasons which aren't clear, tissue that is identical to the endometrium can grow on or in any of the organs in the pelvis. This is called endometriosis. Less commonly it can grow at more distant sites within the abdomen, and very rarely in other unexpected sites such as the lungs. When endometrium grows in the cavity of the womb, its cycle of growth and shedding is expressed as periods.

SOME CAUSES OF PAIN

- Pelvic inflammatory disease (PID) (see page 40)
- Fibroids
- Ovarian cysts (see page 30)
- Complications of early pregnancy
- Cancer (see pages 57 onwards)
- Constipation and other bowel problems

Elsewhere it still grows and regresses but is unable to drain. The growth and release of various irritant substances produces pain, inflammation and scarring.

Endometriotic tissue can form nodules or lumps on the surface and may cause the development of cysts in the ovaries. This growth is cyclical (it alters with the menstrual cycle) which means that symptoms can vary throughout the month and be worse around menstruation.

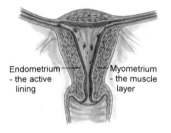

Endometrium
- the active lining

Myometrium
- the muscle layer

There are ligaments which support the womb, and during intercourse these ligaments are stretched. When endometriosis occurs in any of these ligaments this stretching will be painful. Scarring may cause interference with the release of eggs from the ovary, stop them getting from the ovary into the fallopian tube or block the tube.

Characteristically the pain of endometriosis tends to increase in the second half of the menstrual cycle, reaching a peak with the start of the period and then resolving after the period starts. Many cases of endometriosis do not have this classic pattern.

Treatment

Most drug treatments for endometriosis are based on suppressing ovarian activity and hormone release, abolishing the normal cycle:

● **Contraceptive pill:** particularly taken continuously; very little evidence for effectiveness.

DRUGS USED TO TREAT ENDOMETRIOSIS

Progesterones	medroxyprogesterone (Provera)
Anti-oestrogens	danazol (Danol) gestrinone (Dimetriose)
LH-RH analogues	buserelin (Suprecur) goserelin (Zoladex) leuprorelin (Prostap) nafarelin (Synarel)

- **Progesterones:** taken in sufficiently high doses these stop the menstrual cycle (although there may be some spotting) if taken for three or more months; fairly effective. Side effects include nausea, breast tenderness and fluid retention.
- **Anti-oestrogens:** these substances are derived from androgens (related to the male hormone testosterone). This explains many of their side effects, which include acne, hair loss, voice deepening, climacteric symptoms. Very effective, but side effects may limit effectiveness.
- **LH-RH analogues**: these drugs mimic the action of a hormone (luteinising hormone-releasing hormone or LH-RH) released from the hypothalamus. They act on the pituitary gland blocking the release of luteinising hormone (LH) and follicle-stimulating hormone (FSH). The absence of these hormones prevents ovarian activity. Side effects basically result in a temporary menopause.

Surgery

Generally drug treatments suppress endometriosis, but they don't often cure it long term.

This allows relief from symptoms, and where relevant the possibility of pregnancy (which can cure endometriosis).

Women with endometriosis may need surgery because of:

- a failure of medical treatment
- unacceptable side effects
- lack of long-term cure
- structural damage preventing conception.

The definitive surgery for endometriosis is a hysterectomy with removal of both ovaries and tubes, followed by hormone replacement therapy. Such radical treatment is highly effective, but it is appropriate only for women who have completed their families and feel psychologically prepared for its impact. Other surgical treatments involve the removal or destruction of visible endometriotic tissue.

Surgical treatment may be combined with medical therapy. Particularly for more limited surgery, minimally invasive surgical techniques are being used.

ADENOMYOSIS

Adenomyosis is a variant of endometriosis, in which the endometriotic tissue grows in the muscle wall of the womb (myometrium). This condition is very difficult to diagnose with certainty until the womb is examined after a hysterectomy, which is the only really effective form of treatment. Unlike endometriosis, adenomyosis is usually confined to women later in their reproductive years. Symptoms of adenomyosis are painful, often heavy periods.

PELVIC PAIN SYNDROME

Many women experience pelvic pain and pain with intercourse for which no apparent anatomical or pathological cause can be found. Such pain is often thought to have a psychological origin, and to be due to stress, relationship problems, worries about fertility or past experience of sexual abuse. Recurrent episodes of pelvic pain (sometimes associated with such psychological factors) are a feature of pelvic congestion syndrome. This is a controversial condition – some doctors don't believe it exists at all.

There is evidence that at least a proportion of women with otherwise unexplained pelvic pain have dilated veins around the pelvic organs, which are peculiarly sensitive to the high levels of female sex hormones found in these veins. Currently, there is no treatment to change the veins.

Treatment concentrates on decreasing the level of hormones in them, and on psychological support. Suppressing the activity of the ovaries, causing the level of hormones in the ovarian veins to be as low as in the general circulation, is generally effective. This is most easily achieved by treatments with medroxyprogesterone (Provera), which is a synthetic progestogen. Quite high doses need to be given and treatment is usually limited to a few months, following which pain may return. Where the severity is sufficiently severe, hysterectomy, with removal of both ovaries and subsequent non-cyclical hormone replacement therapy, may be appropriate.

IRRITABLE BOWEL SYNDROME

In this condition the bowel has altered muscular activity and sensation. Pelvic pain is produced by muscle spasm and bowel distension (with wind or faeces). The tender distended bowel may cause pain with intercourse when it lies behind the womb at the top of the vagina. More detail about the condition is given in another book in this series (*Understanding your Bowels*). Treatments involve dietary modification, some laxatives, drugs to prevent spasm and avoidance of precipitating factors (such as stress).

KEY POINT

✓ Pain in the abdomen may not be gynaecological in origin

Bladder problems

CYSTITIS

Cystitis simply means inflammation of the bladder, usually as a result of infection. Women are more prone than men or children to develop cystitis, for various reasons:

- the tube which carries the urine out of the bladder (urethra) is shorter in women than men
- the opening of the urethra is nearer the back passage
- because of the first two reasons, intercourse can make it easier for germs to move up the urethra
- use of foam bath and other similar products may allow a reversed flow of water-borne germs into the bladder
- pregnancy, childbirth, hormone deficiency after the menopause, and prolapse can all encourage incomplete bladder emptying which allows germs to multiply
- occasionally a contraceptive diaphragm (especially if ill-fitting) may irritate the urethra or bladder or cause pressure resulting in incomplete emptying – the spermicidal gel may also contribute to the problem.

Infection of the urinary tract (which means the kidneys, via the ureters to the bladder and urethra) may involve all of these organs or be limited to only a part. Most commonly only the bladder is involved. More severe infection involving the kidney and ureter is called pyelonephritis.

The symptoms of cystitis (also called bladder chill) may vary. Particularly in older women, fever may be the only symptom and may result in temporary confusion. More obvious symptoms include:

- dysuria: burning or stinging when passing urine
- frequency: wanting to empty the bladder more often

- lower abdominal pain
- smelly urine.

With pyelonephritis there may also be pain in one side of the back or loin.

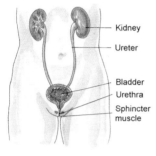

Urinary tract

Treatment

Prevention is always better than cure, so if you are particularly prone to infection it is a good idea to avoid using foam bath and other similar soap products. Prolapse or hormone deficiency may need to be addressed. Try to drink more water or other liquids to flush out the urinary tract. A pharmacist may be able to supply products to be taken by mouth which alter the acidity of urine, making it less irritant to the inflamed bladder lining.

Usually it will be necessary to visit your family doctor (certainly if it's your first episode). This allows the diagnosis to be confirmed by analysis of a sample of urine. A midstream urine test involves wiping the outside of the urethra clean,

starting to pass urine, then catching a part of the middle part of the flow. This portion is least likely to be contaminated by germs from outside and so gives an accurate sample of any germs in the bladder.

If the diagnosis is confirmed, your family doctor is likely to prescribe a course of antibiotics. For simple cystitis this will involve either a single large dose of an antibiotic or a short course lasting about five days. As with all courses of antibiotics it is important to complete the course of treatment and not stop as soon as things improve. For pyelonephritis the course of antibiotics is much longer (usually about a fortnight).

If there has been evidence of pyelonephritis, or recurrent attacks of cystitis, your doctor may arrange investigations to exclude underlying problems with the kidneys, for example, blood tests, scans or X-rays.

INCONTINENCE

There can be incontinence of urine from the bladder, faeces from the bowel or both. Help and treatments are available for both of these common and upsetting problems and you should not be afraid or embarrassed to seek help from your family doctor.

Incontinence of urine

Urinary incontinence is more common after childbirth, and with increasing age (particularly after the menopause) and can be associated with prolapse. It may be due either to a weakness of the valve mechanism at the junction of the bladder and the urethra, or to an overactive bladder muscle (detrusor instability), which pushes urine out of the bladder at times when you don't mean to pass urine. There can often be an overlap in the symptoms from either cause. It may be necessary for your family doctor to refer you to a specialist for advice or tests to establish which type of incontinence you have. This is important, as the valve problem (genuine stress incontinence) is best helped by exercises, weight loss and surgery, whereas detrusor instability is best helped by exercises, bladder drill (in which the bladder is re-trained) or drugs to relax the bladder.

There are various operations for stress incontinence. They are all intended to lift up the bladder neck, which is where the bladder feeds into the urethra. Operations can be done via the vagina, particularly when there is associated prolapse, or via the lower abdomen, when the neck of the bladder is approached from above. There are also minimally invasive surgery options (so-called keyhole surgery). Here either stitches are made using a long needle and then the location of the stitches is checked using a telescope to look into the bladder (cystoscope), or else a viewing tube (laparoscope) is inserted into the abdomen to perform an operation similar to the abdominal approach of conventional surgery mentioned above. Nurse specialists or incontinence advisers can be approached via your district nurse (the receptionist at your surgery can help with this); they can offer special expertise in assessment for aids.

Incontinence of faeces

Faecal incontinence can be very distressing. It is much more common than you may think – people who have it are usually too embarrassed to talk about it, and may be forced into a reclusive lifestyle. They should not be afraid to seek specialist help through their family doctor.

Faecal incontinence is most often caused by injuries to the bowel or nerves leading to the bowel, at the time of childbirth. Such injuries may not be recognised at the time, and subsequent pregnancies may make matters worse. Operations to restore faecal continence may be done abdominally or by incision around the anus (back passage) and rectum. The aim of such surgery is to restore normal anatomy and muscular support to the lower bowel as it passes through the muscles of the pelvic floor.

PROLAPSE

Prolapse of the womb is the condition in which the ligaments supporting the womb become weakened; this is most common in women who have had children and after the menopause.

Weakness in the walls of the vagina can contribute to urinary and faecal continence problems. If the womb itself comes down to the entrance to the vagina, or protrudes from it, it may be uncomfortable or cause local bleeding.

Treatment is by inserting a polythene device – a pessary – which, if effective, can be changed every few months. Vaginal repair or hysterectomy is an effective surgical treatment.

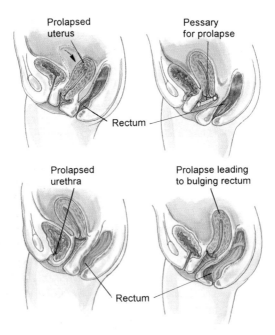

Treatments for prolapse and continence problems

KEY POINTS

✓ Women are particularly prone to bladder infections

✓ Incontinence is not unusual in women who have had several children

Common infections

Vaginal infections may cause discharge, itch and irritation, although sometimes there may be no symptoms. A woman's personal circumstances may indicate an increased risk of sexually transmitted disease. Whenever there is any doubt you should attend a local genitourinary medicine clinic – the phone number and address of your local clinic are in the telephone directory, Yellow Pages and Thomson Directory. You can be seen without a letter from your family doctor, and you will be assured of courteous, confidential and expert treatment. The first episode of any vaginal discharge or irritation will usually require a vaginal examination and probably appropriate tests being taken.

CANDIDA ('THRUSH')

This is an infection with a yeast (*Candida albicans*). It is not generally sexually transmitted, but partners may sometimes also be affected. It usually produces vulval itching and a whitish discharge. Treatment is usually with vaginal tablets (pessaries) or cream, sometimes with tablets taken by mouth. Single-dose treatment is all that's normally needed, and over-the-counter treatment is available.

Some unfortunate women have recurrent attacks of 'thrush'. If you are one of them, you should avoid things that make an attack more likely, such as tights, nylon underwear, and over-zealous hygiene with deodorants and bath additives. In resistant cases your GP may refer you to a specialist.

TRICHOMONAS

This is caused by an organism, *Trichomonas vaginalis*, which is often, but not always, sexually transmitted. It produces a smelly greyish discharge. It is readily treated by an antibiotic (metronidazole or Flagyl).

Treatment for the partner is usually recommended. It is usually wise to be tested for other sexually transmitted diseases – best done by a visit to a local genitourinary medicine clinic.

BACTERIAL VAGINOSIS

This infection produces a similar discharge to trichomonas. It is not sexually transmitted and there is no need for the partner to be examined or treated. Treatment of the affected woman is similar to that for trichomonas. Bacterial vaginosis is not a simple infection, but a disturbance of the normal balance of the organisms normally living in the healthy vagina, allowing pathological organisms to predominate.

CHLAMYDIA

Chlamydia trachomatis is a sexually transmitted organism. Frequently it produces no symptoms. In men it can produce non-specific urethritis (NSU). In women it may lead to pelvic inflammatory disease (see pages 40–1), a vaginal discharge or bleeding with intercourse. Diagnosis is made from swabs (usually from the cervix). Treatment is with antibiotics. As it is sexually transmitted both partners need to be treated and usually should both attend a local genitourinary medicine clinic. Failure to treat this infection can lead to pelvic inflammatory disease, fertility problems or chronic pelvic pain.

GONORRHOEA

Gonorrhoea is less common than it used to be, but it is nevertheless a serious sexually transmitted infection. In men it usually causes a discharge from the urethra at the end of the penis and a burning sensation when passing water. In women, as with chlamydia infection, there are often no symptoms, but when there are they are similar to those experienced with chlamydia. Untreated gonorrhoea can produce exactly the same complications as chlamydia, but in addition can also produce rashes and infections of the joints.

Cases of gonorrhoea should always be referred to a genitourinary medicine clinic, where success of treatment will be confirmed, tests for other sexually transmitted diseases performed and tracing of sexual partner(s) arranged, so that they too can be tested.

HERPES

Herpes is a virus infection – the same virus that causes 'cold sores'. When herpes infection affects the genitals, it is usually transmitted by sexual contact. It is possible to catch the infection from someone with an obvious sore on their genitals. However, many cases of infection occur as a result of virus shed by someone without any visible sore. The virus can also be transmitted from 'cold sores' by oral sex or poor personal hygiene.

Herpes infection usually causes a number of small painful blisters of the genitals, which break down to produce even more painful ulcers. The ulcers then slowly heal over one to two weeks. The first episode of herpes is called a primary attack. Some individuals (about half) may later experience recurrences. These recurrences are usually less severe than primary attacks, although they vary in severity, duration and frequency. Occasionally women are unable to pass urine freely during a primary attack and a catheter may be needed to drain the bladder for a few days. During both primary and recurrent attacks sexual contact should be avoided and sensible hygiene measures adopted. When the severity or frequency of recurrences becomes very troublesome (which happens only in a minority of cases) suppressive treatment to prevent attacks is possible. The anti-viral drug acyclovir (Zovirax) is most effective early in the infection, occasionally used to suppress frequent recurrent attacks.

There has a lot of concern about herpes in pregnancy, but evidence now shows that herpes is only passed to a child during birth if the mother is experiencing an attack at the time of delivery. Any woman with concerns about herpes and childbirth should discuss her worries with her family doctor, midwife or obstetrician.

TREATMENTS FOR HERPES

- Keeping the affected area clean and dry
- Regular bathing in clean water
- Simple painkillers (such as paracetamol)
- Specific anti-viral drug (acyclovir = Zovirax)

GENITAL WARTS

Genital warts are small, warty lumps on the genital skin similar to hand warts, but not so hard and horny (keratinised). Like other warts they are caused by a virus. Different types of wart virus affect different parts of the body, so that the type of wart virus causing hand warts tends not to cause genital warts (and vice versa). Genital warts are generally thought to be sexually transmitted, but the partner may be quite unaffected. Some studies show an association with other sexually transmitted infections, and screening for other infections at a genitourinary medicine clinic is usually advised. It is important to clear any other infections as some infections seem to worsen the warts, or make them difficult to get rid of.

The woman's partner should also be examined (and screened for other infections).

Pregnancy tends to make genital warts worse, making treatment difficult. However, they usually resolve within a few weeks of delivery, even without treatment.

Genital warts (like warts elsewhere) are often difficult to get rid of, and recurrence is common, sometimes requiring repeated courses of treatment.

Topical treatment

- **Podophyllin:** a brown sticky extract from a tropical plant – is applied by a doctor or nurse and washed off a few hours later. Repeated applications are needed.
- **Trichloroacetic acid (TCA):** an acid, related to vinegar, applied as above, and sometimes in combination with podophyllin. Particularly appropriate for keratinised warts.
- **Podophyllotoxin (Warticon):** this product is a purified version of one of the active ingredients of podophyllin. It can be applied by the woman herself (using a mirror) after she has been shown how.

Surgical treatment

- **Cryotherapy:** freezing treatment either with liquid nitrogen, or more usually with a refrigerated 'gun' powered by compressed gas. Some

family doctors may use the former, the latter is usually used in specialist clinics.

- **Surgical excision:** the warts are cut off using tweezers and scissors (usually under local anaesthetic). An extremely effective treatment, which does not produce scarring. Usually confined to very resistant warts or where there are only a few of them.

Women who have or have had genital warts are often advised that they need to have more frequent cervical smears. This is based on the assumption that there is a higher risk of cervical cancer, which we now know is incorrect. The safe policy is, however, to have a smear every three years.

PELVIC INFLAMMATORY DISEASE (PID)

This means infection of the womb and/or tubes or ovaries. Infection of the tubes is sometimes referred to as salpingitis. It is almost always related to sexual activity (which means that women who are not in a relationship very rarely get it), and it is often due to sexually transmitted organisms.

Germs which infect the vagina or cervix manage to get into the upper genital tract, causing infection there. Symptoms are of lower abdominal pain, menstrual irregularity, vaginal discharge, fever and pain with intercourse. Unfortunately some women may have PID without experiencing any symptoms. Untreated it may cause damage to tubes, resulting in fertility problems.

Occasionally it can develop into a pelvic abscess, requiring surgical treatment. Sometimes PID is diagnosed wrongly. Doctors should be careful about labelling frequent episodes of pain as PID, when they may be due to other causes (see page 32). Women who have not had a sexual relationship rarely develop it.

Treatment is with painkillers – usually non-steroidal anti-inflammatory drugs (NSAIDs) and antibiotics. A variety of antibiotics may be used often in combination.

ANTIBIOTICS USED IN TREATMENT OF PID

- Metronidazole (Flagyl)
- Tetracyclines:
  oxytetracycline
  doxycycline (Vibramycin)
  Detelo
- Erythromycin
- Penicillins:
  co-amoxiclav (Augmentin)
  amoxycillin (Amoxil)

HIV, AIDS AND SAFE SEX

The human immunodeficiency virus (HIV) is a virus transmitted by sexual acts or by contact with infected blood or blood products, or passed from mother to child during pregnancy, delivery or breast-feeding. It was first recognised among homosexuals and intravenous drug abusers; it is now found in heterosexual people too. Male-to-female and female-to-male transmission is increasingly important in the spread of HIV. The virus infects and damages white blood cells, which are part of the body's immune system – the mechanism for fighting infection.

People infected with HIV (HIV positive) may be less able to fight infection and so are affected by many infections and diseases which are uncommon in the healthy population. When an HIV positive person has some of these problems they are said to have **a**cquired **i**mmune **d**eficiency **s**yndrome (AIDS).

Is he HIV positive?

Though AIDS is not as rapidly fatal as was thought at first, the outlook for people affected with AIDS is poor as it is (to a lesser extent) for those infected with HIV. Any woman who is concerned about HIV or AIDS should contact a health adviser in a genitourinary medicine clinic, or contact the National AIDS Helpline (see Useful Addresses on page 66).

Tests for HIV infection are available (after proper counselling) from genitourinary medicine clinics.

Becoming infected with HIV by blood or blood products is a particular concern for health professionals, certain groups of patients and intravenous drug abusers (who should avoid sharing needles).

Most women will be more concerned about the risk of transmission through sex, and how to avoid that risk. It is an unfortunate fact that transmission of HIV from a man to a woman is more likely than from a woman to a man.

Sexual abstinence is one answer, but hardly very practical. Avoidance of casual sex with strangers and the use of barrier methods of contraception (male or female condoms) will limit risk in a new relationship.

Although barrier methods offer the best available protection from HIV, they are not the most reliable methods of contraception – you would be well advised to use barrier methods as well as another reliable method such as the contraceptive pill.

It is not possible to tell just from looking whether someone is affected by HIV – you could be at risk from any new sexual partner.

KEY POINTS

✓ Some quite common genital infections cause no symptoms

✓ You can consult your local genitourinary medicine clinic without being referred by your family doctor

✓ Sometimes your partner should be tested as well

✓ HIV can be spread by sexual contact between men and women

Breast problems

ANATOMY

The breasts are formed from several different tissues and are important in sexual activity as well as in breast-feeding.

The nipple is the point at which the milk ducts come to the surface together. It has erectile tissue in it which responds to changes in temperature and sexual arousal. The pigmented skin around it is called the areola. Its size and colour vary considerably from one woman to another. Dotted around the areola are small bumps (Montgomery's tubercles), which may become more prominent in pregnancy.

Breast tissue is made up of milk-producing glands grouped together like bunches of grapes. These are held together by connective tissue and covered by a layer of fatty tissue. The size of the breasts is very variable and of no practical importance. Small breasts are fine for breast-feeding.

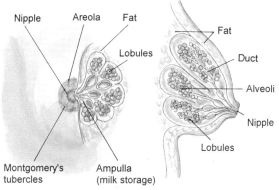

Nipple   Areola   Fat

Fat

Lobules

Duct

Alveoli

Nipple

Montgomery's tubercles

Ampulla (milk storage)

Lobules

The structure of breast tissue

Nipples

The nipples are prone to skin disorders, like any other area of skin. Eczema is quite common and may be confined to the nipple and areola. It is easily treated but should always be diagnosed by your doctor to exclude any of the similar looking but rarer and more serious conditions. In older women Paget's disease of the nipple starts with dry, crusty skin but can progress to a form of cancer. Your family doctor may refer you to a breast specialist or dermatologist (skin specialist) for advice.

Crusting or weeping, or milk or blood coming from the nipple, should always be reported to your family doctor.

Breast infections

Women who are pregnant or breast-feeding, or who have had children, are prone to breast infection. It is rare in women who have never had children. Nipples may be infected with thrush, causing soreness, cracks and bleeding. Your midwife or family doctor will be able to advise you on treatment. Breast abscesses and mastitis usually start with a sore, red, tender area on one breast, accompanied by a temperature or a 'flu-like illness. Antibiotics are very effective and safe to take while you continue to breast-feed, but work best when started early.

Breast pain/tenderness

Most women experience some breast tenderness as part of the menstrual cycle. The increased level of progesterone in the second half of the cycle (from ovulation to menstruation) is thought to stimulate breast tissue, causing enlargement, aching and tenderness. This tenderness can be treated by:

- avoiding caffeine
- herbal diuretics
- vitamin B_6 (pyridoxine).

There is no scientific evidence that these remedies work. Oil of evening primrose (Efamast) is now available over the counter or on prescription. It can be used for the treatment of cyclical breast pain. It takes up to eight weeks to be effective. It is expensive, so if you feel no benefit after taking it for three months then you should probably stop.

Breast pain without a breast lump is rarely serious, but if it is non-cyclical or very distressing then you should consult your family doctor. Sometimes breast pain can be due to problems outside the breast – shingles pain, indigestion or pain referred from the back or chest.

Breast lumps

Many women have quite lumpy breast tissue and this is normal. It is very useful to examine your breasts occasionally (perhaps after a period), so that you become familiar with their outline and texture, enabling you to be able to recognise anything unusual like a lump. Diffusely lumpy breasts don't usually require any treatment, but if they are painful you may need advice.

If you become aware of a nodular, lumpy area in an otherwise normal breast or a breast lump, you should consult your family doctor as soon as convenient. She will examine both breasts, often while you are sitting and again when you are lying down. She'll also check under your arms, where small amounts of breast tissue and lymph nodes lie. She will note the size, texture and position of any lump. Such an examination can give valuable clues about the cause and nature of any lump. You may be referred to a specialist at your local hospital for an X-ray, further examination or other tests, or your family doctor may ask you to come back and see her again in a couple of weeks.

AT THE BREAST CLINIC

If you are referred by your family doctor you may see a breast physician or surgeon. They will want to examine your breasts again and arrange an X-ray (mammogram) and other tests.

The following are the most common tests.

● **Ultrasound:** helps to differentiate between solid lumps and fluid-filled breast cysts.
● **Mammography:** a mammogram is an X-ray of the breasts (see Breast screening on page 61). It can be used both for screening and for getting more detailed information about a lump which has already been found. During the X-ray (under a local anaesthetic) a fine wire is sometimes inserted into the lump, making it easier to find and remove at surgery.
● **Cyst aspiration**: fluid-filled breast cysts can be punctured, the fluid drained and sent for laboratory examination.
● **Biopsy:** using a local anaesthetic a special needle is inserted into the lump and a small piece of tissue removed. If the lump is small or ill-defined the needle may be guided by ultrasound or X-rays. Usually it will take a few days to get laboratory reports back, though sometimes examination of cyst fluid can be done the same day.

Breast lumps can be either benign (harmless) or malignant (cancerous). Most are benign.

A fibroadenoma is sometimes called a 'breast mouse' because they are often very mobile and seem to move about if pressed.

They don't need to be removed, but can be removed under general anaesthetic if they are large or troublesome or if there is any doubt about their nature.

BENIGN BREAST LUMPS

- Solid lumps (fibroadenoma) – nodules of fibrous tissue
- Fluid-filled breast cysts

A breast cyst is effectively treated by puncturing it and draining it with a needle and syringe. Sometimes they come back after drainage, so you may be asked to return for a further check-up.

If your tests show the breast lump is a cancer or has the potential to become cancerous you will be admitted to hospital to remove the lump. This is done under a general anaesthetic. Usually only the lump needs to be removed (lumpectomy).

Removal of the whole breast (mastectomy) is sometimes advisable or necessary, depending on the size and position of the lump. The lymph glands in the armpit may be removed. Your surgeon will discuss the options with you beforehand.

Once the lump has been removed the tissue will be examined in the laboratory. Further treatment may be advised. This may mean

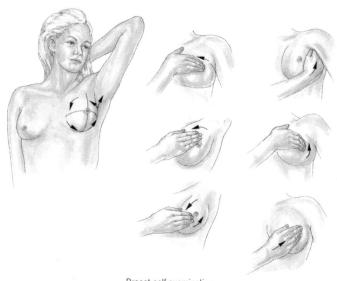

Breast self-examination

chemotherapy (drug treatment) or radiotherapy (X-ray treatment). Further information is available from the addresses given on page 66.

BREAST AWARENESS

This means recognising the nature of your breasts, how that changes with your menstrual cycle, with pregnancy and over the years. If you are breast aware you will notice much sooner any lump that develops. Earlier detection means that earlier diagnosis and treatment are possible, meaning that the results are likely to be better.

You should remember that the vast majority of all breast lumps noticed by women are benign and not malignant, but you should report any concerns promptly to your family doctor.

KEY POINTS

✓ Breast size is very variable – for breast-feeding, size does not matter

✓ It is quite normal to experience breast tenderness at some time in the menstrual cycle

✓ Most breast lumps are not cancerous

✓ If you are aware of how your breasts normally feel, you will soon notice any lump that develops

✓ Don't hesitate to consult your doctor about any unusual pain or suspicious lump

---

Psychosexual problems

Difficulties in enjoying or performing sexual intercourse are very common and most couples will experience temporary problems at some time in their relationship. Some of these problems arise because of physical symptoms related to the genital organs.

Women may experience pain during penetration (superficial dyspareunia) or during intercourse (deep dyspareunia – see page 29). Deep dyspareunia is usually due to inflammation of pelvic organs, whereas superficial dyspareunia is more often due to vaginal inflammation such as that due to local infection (see Common infections, page 37).

Men can find their ability to get an erection and maintain it is affected by certain conditions – diabetes and circulation problems are common causes of loss of potency.

Where there is no direct physical cause to explain sexual difficulties, we use the term psychosexual problem.

Often physical and psychological factors are intertwined. For instance, women may feel less receptive after childbirth when initial attempts are uncomfortable. Unless their partner is understanding, it may then become difficult to relax and enjoy sex for some time afterwards. Loss of enjoyment of sex may arise from decreased sexual appetite – loss of libido.

Many women do not reach orgasm (climax) every time they make love, but a change from what is usual for you may indicate that help is needed.

Psychosexual counsellors may be either doctors or trained therapists with a non-medical background. Help is available through the NHS, private counsellors or counselling organisations such as

Relate (formerly the Marriage Guidance Council). Your family doctor is a useful first port of call. She can listen to your story and may offer a physical examination, which might suggest a cause. Simple advice can be effective, especially if the problem is recent.

Your doctor may also be able to recommend a psychosexual counsellor. Doctors or counsellors in this field undergo a prolonged period of training. If you see someone outside the NHS, always ask about their relevant qualifications before consulting them.

Most counsellors will want to see both partners together, although in some circumstances it may be possible to work with just one of you. Whatever the initial cause of the difficulties in enjoying sex it is often helpful to start back at basics, and a common approach is to initially place a total ban on sexual intercourse.

Then you start with simple non-sexual touching, stroking and massage, gradually extending the range of experience with weekly 'homework' exercises until full intercourse is resumed. There are also techniques to help if your partner has a problem – poor erection, ejaculating ('coming') either too quickly or not at all. Don't be afraid to discuss these intimate problems with either your family doctor or family planning doctor or nurse.

KEY POINTS

✓ Many couples will have a sexual problem at some point in their relationship

✓ Don't hesitate to ask for advice from your doctor or a trained counsellor

Menopause – the climacteric

The menopause is a woman's last period. She can only know it's her last one with hindsight when she hasn't had another one subsequently. The often turbulent troubles which many women experience in the months or years leading up to the menopause and afterwards are technically referred to as the climacteric, often known as the 'change of life' or just the 'change'.

MENSTRUAL PROBLEMS

Some women have no period problems leading up to the climacteric. They simply carry on with regular periods until these end abruptly. Often, though, there may be a few months (occasionally years) of irregular, frequent, prolonged or heavy periods. The management of such problems will depend on individual factors – particularly the woman's age, associated symptoms, contraceptive needs, and so on. Menstrual problems can often be helped by hormone replacement therapy (HRT). Failing this, treatment may be along the lines discussed in the section on heavy or frequent periods (see page 24).

COMMON SYMPTOMS OF THE CHANGE

- Hot flushes
- Night sweats
- Sleep disturbance
- Irritability
- Mood swings
- Depressive symptoms
- Loss of libido (sex drive)
- Vaginal dryness
- Bladder symptoms

SYMPTOMS OF THE CHANGE

Our bodies weren't 'designed' to survive as long as they usually do these days. Our life expectancy is now such that many organs show ageing effects. In women the ovaries gradually become depleted of eggs, ovarian activity ceases, periods stop and high levels of pituitary hormones try in vain to drive the ovaries back to work. These effects are largely caused by the lack of oestrogen from the ovary.

HORMONE REPLACEMENT THERAPY (HRT)

Generally symptoms of the change can be controlled or abolished by using exogenous (from outside the body) oestrogen in the form of HRT. A few years after oestrogen HRT was introduced doctors realised that oestrogen alone could have a harmful effect on the endometrium, leading to a risk of cancer. Now we know that women need to take the other female hormone, progesterone, together with the oestrogen for a few days every so often. Initially this was added for about ten days every month. Such cyclical HRT has an effect like the combined contraceptive pill, resulting in a monthly withdrawal bleed. For women before the menopause this is fine – it often helps to regulate their periods. For postmenopausal women, though, it can be a nuisance to carry on having periods well into their fifties and possibly sixties. The progesterone doesn't need to be taken every month or cyclically. Particularly in women who are in their mid-fifties (or older) or those finding the withdrawal bleeds troublesome there are now other options. Preparations that contain both progesterone and oestrogen taken every day, and preparations in which the progesterone is taken only for a few days once every three months are now available.

One of the main reasons why women discontinue HRT has been the bleeding. Hopefully the newer preparations will allow more women to benefit from long-term therapy.

Apart from suppressing the symptoms of the climacteric, HRT offers other benefits:

- protection against osteoporosis
- improved general well-being
- satisfactory libido

- maintenance of vaginal skin
- maintenance of bladder lining, helping to prevent some bladder symptoms
- protection against the increased risk of strokes and heart attacks which applies to women after the menopause.

There is no reason why women going through the change should suffer in silence. Help is available from your family doctor, family planning or well woman clinic, gynaecologist and menopause clinic.

There are concerns about the adverse effects of HRT. It is true that there is some evidence of a small increase in the risk of breast cancer. Against this you should weigh the protection from some other cancers and all of the advantages above. Overall, women taking HRT are likely to live longer and remain healthier too. There are very few genuine reasons why women should not take HRT (contraindications). Having high blood pressure and treatment for high blood pressure are not contraindications. Some women will prefer to experience a physiological or non-medicalised climacteric and menopause.

There are so many different preparations of HRT that there is bound to be one that suits every woman. If the first preparation used doesn't suit, try another rather than give up. HRT can be given as tablets, implants, patches or gel. Some women have problems (referred to as tachyphylaxis) which means that they become effectively immune to the oestrogen and need higher and higher doses.

Women using implants or patches who have not had a hysterectomy will still need to take cyclical progesterone, which can be in the form of tablets or patches as well. You can refer to *Understanding the*

HRT – PREPARATIONS AVAILABLE

Tablets
Taken daily, usually packaged in some type of calendar pack

Implants
Oestrogen pellets inserted under the skin either at the time of hysterectomy or subsequently under a local anaesthetic. These are replaced about every six months (varies according to individual and dose)

Patches
Stick-on patches containing hormones which can be absorbed across intact skin

Gel
A measured amount of a gel is applied to the skin (like a moisturiser) and rubbed in

Menopause and HRT for discussion of alternative treatments.

SPECIAL PROBLEMS AFTER HYSTERECTOMY

When a hysterectomy is performed the woman has effectively had her last period (or menopause). If the ovaries are removed at the same time, and she had not previously reached the menopause, HRT will usually be needed. It should be started straightaway, or severe symptoms may be experienced. For women who have had a hysterectomy where the ovaries are not removed (ovarian conservation) there are two particular problems:

1 Often the ovaries seem to stop working earlier than might otherwise be expected. If this results in symptoms, the woman may realise what is going on and seek help.

2 A woman who has had a hysterectomy may not experience any recognisable symptoms when her ovaries cease to work.

Both of these problems may result in women before the age of the natural menopause developing the bone loss, heart attack and stroke risks associated with lack of oestrogen, without realising there's a problem. Women who have had a hysterectomy with ovarian conservation should ask their family doctor to check their hormone level at least every few years.

If a woman in this situation experiences symptoms she should certainly seek advice.

One of the benefits of having had a hysterectomy is that HRT is simplified. The progesterone which is required to protect the endometrium from the harmful effects of oestrogen is not needed. HRT after hysterectomy should therefore be based on oestrogen only (as tablets, patches or implants). Cyclical side effects such as unwanted bleeding are avoided.

KEY POINTS

✓ Hormone replacement therapy (HRT) can help to control or abolish unpleasant symptoms

✓ Some women have no problems with the change of life

✓ You don't have to suffer in silence

After the menopause

POSTMENOPAUSAL BLEEDING

Although postmenopausal bleeding is usually not due to anything sinister, it is occasionally due to malignant disease (cancer) within the genital tract. Postmenopausal bleeding is usually regarded as any bleeding six months or more after a woman's periods have ended.

For this reason any episode of postmenopausal bleeding should initially be regarded as suspicious and the advice of your family doctor sought. Usually your doctor will refer you to a gynaecologist. The role of the gynaecologist is to carry out tests for cancer and, if the tests are positive, to arrange for treatment.

More than 90 per cent of women with postmenopausal bleeding do not have cancer. In order to be able to assess the cervix and endometrium either your family doctor or gynaecologist will:

- check that your last smear was up-to-date and satisfactory
- do a vaginal examination to check the state of the cervix and vagina
- assess the endometrium.

ASSESSING THE ENDOMETRIUM

- Endometrial biopsy
- Ultrasound scan
- Hysteroscopy
- Dilatation and curettage (D&C)

The condition of the endometrium, the lining of the uterus, is best assessed by examination of a small piece of it under a microscope. This can be obtained by a minor procedure in hospital. A simple suction tube may be used passed through the cervix, but sometimes a viewing instrument is used (see hysteroscopy, p.27) or a minor operation called dilatation and curettage is preferred.

Which method is used to assess the endometrium will depend on the circumstances. Particularly if an ultrasound scan or simple endometrial biopsy is used, it may be possible for this to be dealt with during a single outpatient visit.

Non-sinister (benign) causes for postmenopausal bleeding include:

- cervical polyps (small finger-like overgrowths of tissue) – these can also occur in women before the menopause
- endometrial polyps (similar growths within the womb)

- atrophic vaginitis (thin vaginal skin due to hormone deficiency after the menopause).

If any of these is found the treatment is relatively simple. Polyps may be dealt with during an outpatient visit, or occasionally as a day-case procedure. Atrophic vaginitis is treated by conservative measures, HRT or topical oestrogens (this means HRT to the vagina only, as cream, pessaries or a hormone-releasing vaginal ring).

In the unlikely event of a cancer of either the cervix or endometrium being discovered, treatment may involve either a hysterectomy (with removal of both ovaries and tubes,

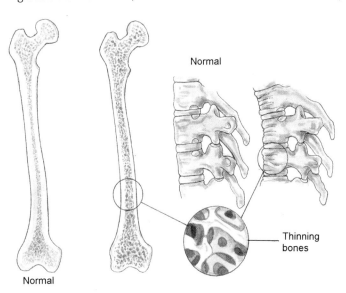

Normal

Normal

Thinning bones

Thinning of the interior of bones such as the femur makes them lighter and more fragile.
The bones of the spine may be crushed causing pain and loss of height

and sometimes some of the lymph nodes around them), or radiotherapy. Generally there is a good chance of complete cure. After treatment, long-term follow-up to detect recurrence is normal.

OSTEOPOROSIS

Osteoporosis – thinning of the bones – is an inevitable part of the ageing process for women and men. Minerals, especially calcium, are lost, weakening the structure of the bones and leading to more easily broken bones. Osteoporosis is generally:

- more severe in women than in men
- more severe in white women than in black
- more severe in smokers
- more likely in people who are less active
- more likely in thinner people
- more common in those with a family history of osteoporosis.

OSTEOPOROSIS

The thinning of bones that occurs after the menopause, which results in:

- a greater risk of broken bones
- loss of height
- other associated complications

Osteoporosis can be treated or prevented by HRT (see page 51 and *Understanding the Menopause and HRT*). It can also be treated by calcium supplements and other drugs. It can be detected by a special X-ray technique called bone densitometry.

The technique is becoming more widely available and increasingly is being used for selective screening. Once osteoporosis has been diagnosed in this way, densitometry may be used to measure the effect of treatment.

KEY POINTS

✓ You should tell your doctor about any post-menopausal bleeding

✓ Osteoporosis can be treated or prevented by hormone replacement therapy (HRT)

Cancer and screening

Malignancies or cancers are growths of tissue which are not controlled by the normal mechanisms that control the growth of cells. Cancers have the ability to spread out from the tissue in which they start out (invasion); they can spread either into adjacent tissues or via blood and lymph vessels to distant organs (metastasis).

Cancers are classified into:

- carcinomas – the malignant cells originally come from either skin or lining tissue
- sarcomas – the cells come from connective, fibrous tissue or bone
- lymphomas – the cells come from the lymph nodes
- leukaemias – the cells come from blood cells and bone marrow.

The vast majority of gynaecological and breast cancers are carcinomas.

Occasionally sarcomas occur and very rarely lymphomas are found. When doctors talk about cancer (either among themselves or to patients) they may use a variety of terms. Some of these are intended to soften the impact, some are really to allow doctors to talk about cancer without patients understanding. The different terms are:

- growth (technically not always malignant but a common euphemism for cancer)
- malignancy
- tumour (may be malignant or benign but again a common euphemism)
- mitotic lesion
- cancer
- carcinoma (or other words ending in -oma).

Cancers can affect any organ of the body, though some are much more common than others. In this chapter we will concentrate on cancers of the breast and gynaecological organs.

VULVA

Cancer of the vulva (the skin around the opening to the vagina) is uncommon. It almost always occurs in older women (over 70). It is usually starts off as either an ulcer or a small lump, sometimes like a large wart. Any woman, particularly an older woman, who notices any suspicious lump or ulcer on the vulva should report it to her family doctor as soon as possible. Sadly, many older women don't mention it to their doctor until too late when the tumour has become large and has often spread to nearby lymph nodes. In such cases the results of treatment are often disappointing. In early disease removal of an area of skin from the vulva can completely remove the tumour, but in later cases treatment needs to be more radical – if treatment is possible at all.

In the vast majority of cases there is no obvious cause for cancer of the vulva. Occasionally, though, it can arise in certain skin conditions affecting the vulva.

CERVIX

Cancer of the cervix can occur in women of any age, but it most commonly affects women in middle age (40 onwards). We know that some groups of women are slightly more likely to develop this problem, but is important to remember that cervical cancer can occur in any woman. As the cervix is at the top of the vagina, a tumour is not normally visible, but symptoms can be:

- persistent vaginal discharge
- bleeding:
  between periods
      (intermenstrual bleeding)
  after sexual intercourse
      (postcoital bleeding)
  after the menopause
      (postmenopausal bleeding)
- pain:
  with intercourse
  at other times.

A woman with such symptoms should report them to her family doctor, who will then usually perform a vaginal examination and perhaps a cervical smear. Unless the doctor is quite certain there is nothing sinister she may refer the woman to a gynaecologist for further assessment. If there is cancer of the cervix the diagnosis will usually be obvious to the gynaecologist, but it is usually necessary to take a piece of tissue (biopsy) to confirm the diagnosis. A detailed examination under a general anaesthetic, together with combinations of X-rays and scans, may be needed to confirm any spread of tumour and indicate what treatment is needed. Depending on age, nature, size and extent of the tumour, treatment may involve one method or a combination of several. Very rarely (and in younger women) even more radical treatment is sometimes needed.

TREATMENT OF CERVICAL CANCER

- Simple hysterectomy
- Extended hysterectomy (with sampling of lymph nodes in the pelvis)
- Radiotherapy
- Chemotherapy

Early cancers (and also precancerous changes detected by cervical screening) can be treated with a high chance of complete cure. It is most important to mention any such symptoms to your doctor as soon as you notice them.

ENDOMETRIUM

Cancer of the endometrium almost always arises in women who are postmenopausal. It is slightly more common in women who are obese, have diabetes, and have no children. It usually reveals itself by postmenopausal bleeding (or by intermenstrual bleeding in women in their forties) (see page 29). If it is recognised early it can be treated with very high rate of cure by simple hysterectomy with removal of the ovaries and tubes.

Sometimes, if the tumour has started to invade far into the muscle layer of the womb (myometrium) then additional treatment with radiotherapy and/or hormones may be needed.

OVARY

Cancer of the ovary can occur in girls or women of any age. The most common ovarian cancers occur in postmenopausal women. Some of the less common kinds of tumour occur in younger women. There are more types of tumour of the ovary than any other organ in the body. In such a small book as this it would be impossible to cover all of these tumours, so we will only mention the more common malignant cysts (carcinomas of the ovary).

Women who develop the rarer tumours – particularly younger women – should discuss issues with their gynaecologist or family doctor (or consult one of the sources listed on page 66).

As the ovary is an internal organ, cancers occurring in it may not produce symptoms until they are well established. This unfortunately often means that they have spread widely. When tumours are limited to the ovary there is a reasonable hope of curative surgery, and often additional chemotherapy. Unfortunately many ovarian tumours don't produce symptoms until it is too late.

Ovarian cancer may produce a variety of abdominal symptoms – indigestion, acid reflux, constipation, pain, abdominal swelling. Whenever an ovarian tumour is suspected in an older woman she will usually be referred to a gynaecologist. An ultrasound scan will help make the diagnosis.

After blood tests and X-rays, an exploratory operation is usually carried out to confirm the diagnosis. If a cancer is found, extensive surgery is usually needed to remove the womb, tubes and ovaries and also any visible deposits of tumour spread. Subsequently chemotherapy is likely to be needed.

Cancer of the ovary is slightly more common in women who have never been pregnant. It is less common in women with children and very much less common in women who have previously taken the combined contraceptive pill for any length of time.

As with the treatment of all cancers, after treatment for all gynaecological cancers long-term follow-up (usually for about five years) is normal.

WHAT IS SCREENING?

Screening for disease is the process where everyone in a group thought to be at risk for a particular disease or condition is tested for it.

To screen effectively, both the condition being tested and the test must meet certain criteria. The condition should be relatively common and it should be known that early detection and treatment have a better outcome than waiting until the condition is obvious or more severe. The test should be simple, so that as many people as possible in the target group will agree to be tested. It should be reasonably cheap and should be reliable.

One difficulty common to all screening tests currently available is that they may sometimes miss some people who are actually affected, offering false reassurance (false negatives).

They also tend to produce positive results in some people who don't actually have the condition, causing false alarms and needless worries (false positives). These people end up needing further tests and assessments before finally being given the all clear.

An example of screening applied to the whole UK population is the examination of all babies in their first six weeks of life by health visitors, doctors and midwives, to detect dislocated hips.

Earlier detection of this problem, leading to earlier treatment, prevents later difficulties with walking.

Women in the UK are currently offered two screening tests – cervical smears to detect abnormalities of the cervix (to prevent later cervical cancer) and mammography to detect early cancer of the breast. Two other conditions which are sometimes screened for – both still on an experimental basis – are osteoporosis and ovarian cancer.

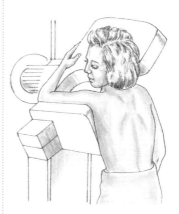

Mammography

Screening for breast cancer

Cancer of the breast is not usually detected until the woman or her doctor finds a lump in her breast (see page 44). By the time a lump can be felt in the breast, the cancer has been there for some years. Mammography in the NHS is at an interval of two or three years. Detection of smaller earlier tumours by screening offers the hope of removing the tumour before it has had a chance to spread to other parts of the body and when local treatment is likely to be more effective.

A mammogram is a special X-ray of the breast. Each breast in turn is gently squeezed between two Perspex plates and X-ray pictures are taken. Invitations are sent to all women from the age of 50 onwards for a mammogram every two years.

PROBLEMS WITH MAMMOGRAPHY

- Not all women take up the offer of the test
- It can sometimes be quite uncomfortable
- Some very small tumours can spread beyond the breast before they can be detected by mammography
- Most women called for further tests will not be found to have cancer

Women over 65 are not routinely invited as experience shows they are less likely to attend, but they will be welcome at the breast screening service if they express an interest. The test may be done at your local hospital or in a mobile unit.

The mammograms are examined by a radiologist, and any woman with an abnormal X-ray will be invited back for a second test where two pictures of each breast are taken and further investigation is offered.

Screening for cervical cancer

The screening test used against cervical cancer is the cervical smear. This involves an internal examination by a doctor or specially trained nurse. An instrument (speculum) is inserted into the vagina, to allow the doctor or nurse to see the cervix. A wooden or plastic spatula is used to scrape loose surface cells from the cervix. The cells are then spread onto a glass microscope slide and sprayed with alcohol to dry them. The sample is then sent to a pathology laboratory, where a technician stains the cells with special dye (Papanicolaou stain) and examines each slide under the microscope looking for abnormal cells (dyskaryosis).

It is believed that cervical cancer develops slowly over many years and that in most cases early changes can be detected on cervical smears before cancer actually develops. Treatment at this early stage is thought to prevent the later development of cancer of the cervix.

Smears are either negative (reassuring), unsatisfactory (not a sufficient sample to give a reliable answer) or abnormal. Some abnormalities are so minor that the test can just be repeated a few months later without any need for referral to

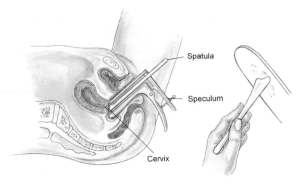

Spatula

Speculum

Cervix

Taking a cervical smear

a specialist. Occasionally some minor abnormalities may be due to infection and can return to normal after treatment with appropriate antibiotics.

More significant abnormalities are shown in the table, together with the degree of abnormality of the cervix which is usually associated with them. It is important to bear in mind that there is not a perfect agreement between the smear grading and the actual degree of abnormality in the cervix. The abnormalities of the cervix which are thought to precede the development of cancer are called cervical intraepithelial neoplasia (CIN). Women aged 20 and over are called for smears every three to five years (depending on local policy), until they are 65.

If your smears until 65 have been normal then problems are unlikely in the future. A computerised register is held in each district of women in the screening programme to ensure that women are called at the right times for smears.

Common practice is to repeat inflammatory smears and those showing mild dyskaryosis in case they have returned to normal without treatment. Women whose smears show moderate dyskaryosis or worse will be referred to a specialist gynaecologist for colposcopy. This is a more detailed visual examination of the cervix, using a special microscope and special stains to detect abnormal cells. Usually the gynaecologist will be able to identify the area of the

SMEARS AND CERVICAL ABNORMALITIES

Smear result	Cervical abnormality
Negative	Normal cervix
Inflammatory	May mean some infection of the cervix or vagina
Mild dyskaryosis	CIN 1
Moderate dyskaryosis	CIN 2
Severe dyskaryosis	CIN 3
Malignant cells	Possibly cancer
Abnormal glandular cells	Usually only seen in combination with CIN 1–3, occasionally seen on its own, may imply a precancerous change in some of the mucous glands of the cervix

cervix which contains the abnormal cells.

She may need to take a small piece of tissue from that area (biopsy) before arranging treatment at a later date, or it may be possible to treat the area at the first visit. Most treatments can be done under local anaesthetic, although general anaesthetic is occasionally needed. All treatments for CIN are aimed at either destroying or removing the area containing the abnormal cells (excision).

Rarely (particularly if there are other gynaecological problems) a hysterectomy may be offered as treatment for CIN. After the treatment has been completed, follow-up tests are needed to ensure the treatment has worked. These involve either further colposcopy examinations, more frequent smears or a combination.

POSSIBLE TREATMENTS FOR CIN

- **Destructive methods**
  cryocautery – freezing
  'cold' coagulation – actually heats the tissue to just above 100°C (boiling point)
  laser vaporisation
  electrodiathermy – uses an electric current to burn the tissue
- **Excisional methods**
  knife cone biopsy – now rarely used except for bigger areas
  laser cone – uses a laser to cut a small cone of tissue
  loop excision – uses a hot wire (rather like a cheese wire) to remove a core of tissue

PROBLEMS WITH CERVICAL SCREENING

- Obtaining a smear requires an intimate examination, which may be uncomfortable for some women
- Although the test is fairly inexpensive it is very labour intensive to process and 'operator dependent', giving rise to potential errors
- Most women found to have an abnormal smear would never progress to cervical cancer, but most of these women will remain anxious about their health even after treatment

Screening for ovarian cancer

There is no established screening programme for cancer of the ovary. Research is currently in progress to develop such a programme. Occasionally there can be a particular history of ovarian cancer affecting more than one woman within a family.

Initially researchers have tended to target these women at increased risk for screening. The vast majority of cases of ovarian cancer do not arise in such 'high-risk' women and so if any programme is to make a significant impact on deaths from ovarian cancer it will (eventually) have to be applicable to all women.

Current methods of screening are based on three techniques:

- regular pelvic examinations by a gynaecologist
- ultrasound scans to assess the size and appearances of the ovaries
- blood tests to measure the levels of 'tumour markers' – these are chemicals known to be present at higher levels in ovarian tumours.

None of these methods will detect all tumours. Each of the tests also has false positives – abnormal results in women who do not have cancer. Most current work is based on a combination of ultrasound scans and blood tests.

Most women currently being screened in this way are involved in one of the research programmes. Occasionally some 'well woman' packages include ovarian cancer screening. Before taking part in such screening women should discuss the implications with their GP or a specialist gynaecologist.

KEY POINTS

- ✓ Unusual bleeding should always be reported to your doctor
- ✓ False positives and false negatives cause anxiety
- ✓ Treatment of abnormal smears is straightforward
- ✓ The earlier cancer is detected, the more likely it is to be successfully treated
- ✓ Women in the UK are currently offered screening tests for cervical cancer and breast cancer

Useful addresses

Amarant Trust
Sycamore House, 5 Sycamore Street,
London EC1Y 0SB
Tel: 020 7608 3222
Fax: 020 7490 2296
Email: amarant@marketforce-
communications.co.uk
Clinic: 80 Lambeth Road,
London SE1 7PW
Tel: 020 7401 3855
Fax: 020 7928 9134

Provides information on hormone
replacement therapy and runs a
private clinic.

Breast Cancer Care
Kiln House, 210 New Kings Road,
London SW6 4NZ
Freephone: 0808 800 6000
Fax: 020 7384 3387
Email: bcc@breastcancercare.org.uk
Website: breastcancercare.org.uk

Specialist breast care nurses provide
practical advice, medical information and support to women
concerned about breast cancer.
Volunteers who have had breast
cancer themselves assist in giving
emotional support to cancer
patients and their partners. Free
leaflets and a prosthesis-fitting
service are also provided.

British Association of Electrolysis Ltd
40 Parkfield Road, Bickenham UB10
8IW
Tel: 0870 1280477
Fax: 0870 1330407
Email: sec@baeltd.ssbusiness.co.uk

Provides a sound, reliable elec-
trolysis service through its
registered members.

British Association for Sexual and Relationship Therapy
PO Box 13686, London SW20 9ZH
Telephone number not available
Email: info@basrt.org.uk
Website: www.basrt.org.uk

British Infertility Counselling Association (BICA)
69 Division Street, Sheffield S1 4GE
Tel: 01342 843880
Fax: 01663 765285
Email: info@bica.net
Website: www.bica.net

Provides a list of counsellors who deal with fertility problems.

Brook Centres
Studio 421, Highgate Studios
51–79 Highgate Road
London NW5 1TL
Tel: 0800 0185 023
Admin: 020 7284 6070
Fax: 020 7284 6050
Email: information@brookcentres.org.uk
Website: www.brook.org.uk

Aims to protect, promote and preserve the sexual and reproductive health of young people by educating them in matters relating to sexual behaviour, contraception, sexually transmitted infections and unwanted pregnancy.

Cancerlink
11–21 North Down Street,
London N1 9BN
Freephone Support Link:
0808 808 0000
Groups Line: 020 7520 2603 (training, information and development for cancer self-help and support groups)
Admin: 020 7833 2818
Fax: 020 7833 4963
Email: cancerlink@cancerlink.org.uk
Website: www.cancerlink.org

CHILD (National Infertility Support Network)
Charter House, 43 St Leonard's Road,
Bexhill-on-Sea TN40 1JA
Tel: 01424 732361
Fax: 01424 731858
Email: office@child.org.uk
Website: www.child.org.uk

This network provides information, advice and a list of local support groups.

Continence Foundation
307 Hatton Square, 16 Baldwins Gardens, London EC1N 7RJ
Helpline: 020 7831 9831 (Mon–Fri 9.30am–4.30pm)
Fax: 020 7404 6876
Email: continence.foundation@dial.pipex.com
Website: www.continence-foundation.org.uk

Has a range of literature for people with continence problems. Callers can speak to nurses with a specialist knowledge of bladder and bowel problems. They also hold a database of services and products throughout the UK.

Family Planning Association
2–12 Pentonville Road, London N1 9FP
Tel: 020 7837 5432
Fax: 020 7837 3042
Website: www.fpa.org.uk

Deals mainly with contraception, but a useful source of up-to-date information about other services and organisations relating to women's health.

Herpes Viruses Association
41 North Road, London N7 9DP
Tel: 020 7609 9061
Website: www.herpes.org.uk

Aims to improve understanding of herpes viruses and help people with herpes viruses. Publishes a quarterly journal, *Sphere*, and leaflets on every aspect of herpes simplex. Organises seminars, social events, workshops and local contacts. Supplies details of self-help and medical treatment for shingles.

Human Fertilisation and Embryology Authority (HFEA)
Paxton House, 30 Artillery Lane, London E1 7LS
Tel: 020 7377 5077
Fax: 020 7377 1871
Website: www.hfea.gov.uk

This statutory government body regulates clinics providing IVF, donor insemination and embryo research. It produces an annual Patient's Guide, with extensive information about all licensed IVF centres in the UK (including their success rates).

ISSUE (The National Fertility Association)
114 Lichfield Street, Walsall WS1 1SZ
Tel: 01922 722888
Fax: 01922 740070
Email: webmaster@issue.co.uk
Website: www.issue.co.uk

This association provides support for people with fertility problems.

Marie Stopes International
153 Cleveland Street, London W1P 5PG
Tel: 0171 574 7400
Fax: 0171 574 7417
Website: www.mariestopes.org.uk

Largest private provider of family planning services in Britain.

Miscarriage Association
c/o Clayton Hospital, Northgate, Wakefield WF1 3JS
Tel: 01924 200799
Fax: 01924 298834
Email: miscarriageassociation@care4free.net
Website: www.miscarriageassociation.org.uk

Provides support and information on all aspects of pregnancy loss.

National AIDS Helpline
Tel: 0800 567123
Fax: 0151 227 4019

National Association for Premenstrual Syndrome
7 Swift's Court, High Street, Seal, Sevenoaks TN15 0EG
Helpline: 01732 760012 (recorded information on counsellors available)
Fax: 01732 760011
Email: naps@pms.org.uk
Website: www.pms.org.uk

Provides help, information and support to PMS sufferers and their families.

National Endometriosis Society
50 Westminster Palace Gardens, Artillery Row, London SW1P 1RL
Helpline: 020 7222 2776 (7–10pm)
Fax: 020 7222 2786
Email: n.info@compuserve.com
Website: www.endo.org.uk

Provides information, support and counselling for women with endometriosis. Publishes quarterly newsletter.

National Infertility Awareness Campaign (NIAC)
PO Box 2106, London W1A 3DZ
Helpline: 0800 716345
Tel: 020 7815 3993

National Osteoporosis Society
PO Box 10, Radstock, Bath BA3 3YB
Helpline: 01761 472721 (Mon
10am–5.30pm, Tues–Fri
9.30am–5.30pm)
Tel: 01761 471771
Fax: 01761 471104
Email: info@nos.org.uk
Website: www.nos.org.uk

Provides advice and support for people with osteoporosis.

British Pregnancy Advisory Service
Austy Manor
Wootton Wawen
Solihull B95 6BX
Helpline: 08457 304030 (8am–9pm
Mon–Fri; 8.30am–6.30pm Sat;
9.30am–2.30pm Sun)
Tel: 020 8682 4001
Fax: 020 8682 4012
Email: comm@bpas.org
Website: www.bpas.org

Positively Women
347–349 City Road, London EC1V 1LR
Helpline: 020 7713 0222
Fax: 020 7713 1020

TAMBA (Twins & Multiple Births Association)
Harnott House, 309 Chester Road,
Ellesmere Port CH66 1QQ
Helpline: 01732 868000 (7–11pm
weekdays, 10am–11pm weekends)
Tel: 0151 348 0020 or 0870 121 4000
Fax: 0151 348 0765 or 0870 121 4001
Email: enquiries@tambahq.org.uk
Website: www.tamba.org.uk

Offers information and support to families with twins, triplets and more and to those involved with their care.

Verity (Polycystic Ovaries Self Help Group)
52–54 Featherstone Street, London
EC1Y 8RT
Email: enquiries@verity-pcos.org.uk
Website: www.verity-pcos.org.uk

Provides information and support for those with polycystic ovaries. Members receive a newsletter, *In Touch*. Organises quarterly support group meetings.

Well Woman Clinics
Look in your local telephone directory and Yellow Pages. These clinics may be run by your GP, by the local family clinic, by private organisations such as Marie Stopes (see above) or by the local hospital.

Women's Aid Federation England

PO Box 391, Bristol BS99 7WS
Tel: 0117 944 4411
Fax: 0117 924 1703
Email: wafe@wafe.co.uk
Website: www.womensaid.org.uk

Provides advice and information services about domestic violence.

Women's Health

52 Featherstone Street
London EC1Y 8RT
Helpline: 0845 125 5254 (Mon–Fri 9.30am–1.30pm)
Tel: 020 7251 6333
Fax: 020 7250 4152
Website:
www.womenshealthlondon.org.uk

Provides information on gynae-cological and sexual health issues, through their helpline and leaflets.

Women's Health Concern

PO Box 2126, Marlow, Bucks SL7 2RY
Helpline: 01628 483612 (hours vary)
Tel: 01628 488065
Fax: 01628 474042

Offers advice and counselling to women with gynaecological and hormonal problems. Publishes books and factsheets (send an s.a.e. for a current list of publications).

Index